The Prestige S...

Barton 2

John Banks
Photography by G H F Atkins

© 2004 J M Banks
ISBN 1 898432 96 1

All rights reserved. Except for normal review purposes no part of this book may be reproduced or utilised in any form or by any means, electrical or mechanical, including photocopying, recording or by an information storage and retrieval system, without the prior written consent of Venture Publications Ltd, Glossop, Derbyshire.

Cover and rear cover: Barton's pride and joy, and possibly the most unusual double-decker ever owned, was No. **861** (**861 HAL**), the lowbridge, low-height Dennis Loline. In these 1960 pictures it is shown ready for its appearance at the 1960 Commercial Motor Show, where it caused a sensation. *(Both: Senior Transport Archive)* Also shown is the familiar logo, widely used after the acquisition of Robin Hood (Coaches) Ltd in October 1961.

Inside front cover: Number **1087** (**SAU 199**) *(upper)* was a Park Royal-bodied lowbridge 53-seater acquired from Nottingham City Transport in 1967. It was among the last handful of double-deckers to enter the Barton fleet. From 1962's second-hand purchases is illustrated *(lower)* former Todmorden Corporation Leyland-bodied Titan PD2/1 No. **943** (**FWT 184**).

Inside rear cover: Barton's ability to rebuild old chassis to up-to-date specification allowed some useful additions to the fleet. Number **736** (**VVO 736**) was originally a 1949 Leyland Tiger PS1/1, No. **551** (**KAL 148**). It lost its body in 1956, its chassis was rebuilt and then rebodied by Willowbrook as a lowbridge 61-seater with platform doors. It was photographed in 1967.

Title page: Such was the demand for travel to Skegness that double-deckers were often employed on Barton's service from Nottingham to the bracing resort, as in this busy scene in Huntingdon Street, outside the bus station, in May 1955. On such occasions, luggage was stored at the front of the lower deck. Number **507** (**JVO 230**) was a 1948 Leyland PD1 with Duple 55-seat lowbridge bodywork.

Opposite page: There was a sizeable second-hand contingent in the Barton fleet. **BCK 938**, which took the Barton fleet number **807**, was a 1947 Leyland Titan PD1, with Leyland lowbridge bodywork, that had come to Barton from Preston Corporation in 1959. It was in the yard at Chilwell, Barton's headquarters, in September 1961. Number **585** (**HL 8613**) alongside was a 1938 Titan TD5 formerly a unit of the West Riding fleet.

Below: In a November 1956 view of Broad Marsh, Nottingham, six Barton vehicles are visible, including two wartime Guy Arabs, one of them - No. **445** (**GNN 706**) rebuilt by Barton; an ex-Leeds AEC Regent, No. **661** (**CNW 910**); a 1949 Duple-bodied Leyland PS1/1, No. **562** (**KAL 382**); one of the 1939 Leyland TD5s, No. **347** (**EVO 711**); and No. **585** (**HL 8613**) again, the ex-West Riding Leyland Titan TD5. Happening upon mixed collections of buses like this was one of the joys of Barton watching in the fifties and sixties.

BARTON
ROBIN HOOD
BARTON
HOME are best!
GLASGOW
ALES best!
CHILWELL
HOME are best!
ALES best!
807
BCK 938
585
HL 8613
KAL 152

Introduction

As will be well known to readers of previous volumes in this series that have drawn on the work of the Nottingham-born photographer G H F Atkins, Geoffrey has made his main task within our hobby the recording on film of The Art of the Coachbuilder. As a young man his ambition was to enter the coachbuilding industry and be involved at close quarters with the craft that so fascinated him. That ambition was never realised and he embarked instead upon a career in local authority administration with Nottingham City Council. All his working life, except for enforced military service during the Second World War, was spent thus: a remarkably stable achievement.

Geoffrey was born in Nottingham in January 1912 and has always lived there: indeed, he still does as these words are being written in the summer of 2003. He has concentrated his transport photography on his local fleets, with occasional forays - mainly during summer holidays in Yorkshire, Lincolnshire, Wales, the West Country and the South-East - further afield. And all this over a period stretching back to his first bus photograph in 1927.

In his pursuit of the offerings of British coachbuilders he could scarcely have had - and on his doorstep at that - a more useful fleet than that of Barton Transport, in which most of the major, and a fair few of the minor, British bodywork manufacturers have been represented, not to mention Barton's own activities in rebuilding as well as the construction of new bodies to their own design.

The companion to this volume, *Barton 1*, published in September 2003, dealt with the Barton single-deck fleet. In general, this one will cover, by means of a chronological survey, the double-deckers in the period encompassing the Leyland TD1 Titan and the enclosed-radiator AEC Regent V and Renown models, which were respectively the first and last Barton "traditional" front-engined buses. The advent of the Titan coincided with Geoffrey Atkins getting into his stride as a bus photographer.

There had been Barton double-deckers before the Titan. In the very early days, before the First World War, there were a Clarkson steamer and a Lacoste-Battman. After the end of that war some Daimler Y chassis with double-deck bodies were used, as were two AECs and a Straker Squire. Some of the Daimlers were modified by Barton and these vehicles had all entered service by 1923. There was then a lull until the bizarre Gilfords of 1929 *(see page 9)*, a further break until the ex-demonstrator Titan in 1932, and a further seven years - broken only by two ex-Campion, of Nottingham, AEC Regents - until the Leyland Titan TD5s of 1939. There were some Titan TD7s in 1940 and a collection of unfrozen AEC Regents and utility

It would take the Barton Leyland double-deck fleet some years to even approach the richness and diversity of the single-deck contingent. The first Titan - a TD1 ex-demonstrator - came in April 1932, and that had been preceded by a pair of LT2 Lions in 1931. Thence the Lion, in LT5, LT7 and LT8 form, with occasional help from the Tiger, was the Lancashire manufacturer's great success in the Nottinghamshire independent's fleet. Leyland double-deckers - TD5 and TD7 Titans - reappeared as late as 1939/40: thereafter it would be 1947 before the next new double-deckers - the famous Duple-bodied PD1s - appeared. There were, however, large numbers of second-hand Titans from a variety of sources. A hint of the glorious array of single-deckers that the TD5 and TD7 Titans would join is given in this 1935 view of 15 "BAL" registered Lions and one Tiger. The writer is grateful to Mr J S Sonley, of Truro, for the information that the original of this picture, measuring 23½ins by 10ins, used to hang in Barton's Chilwell office. (John Banks Collection)

*Before 1931, when the provisions of the Road Traffic Act, 1930 took effect, there had been considerably less official control over what bus operators did - a situation exploited to the full by Mr T H Barton in his many and varied experiments, rebuildings, lengthenings and general striving to carry as many people as possible at the smallest cost. From 1931 matters were under much tighter control and a direct result was that Barton turned to Leyland for a virtually standardised fleet. Although, as we have seen, it would be the turn of the decade from the thirties to the forties before double-deckers made their mark, the standards of finish and maintenance on the single-deckers of the thirties was second to none. Number **162** (**VO 9462**), a 1933 Leyland-bodied 35-seat Lion LT5, is seen when brand new. (John Banks Collection)*

Guy Arabs during the Second World War. In the early stages of that conflict 26 second-hand Leyland Titan TD1s, none newer than 1931, were purchased from a variety of operators: Chatham & District, Todmorden Corporation, Cleethorpes Corporation, London Transport, Southern National, Tyneside Tramways, Western SMT and Birkenhead Corporation. They were all rebodied, remarkably, given that this was at the height of the war, to full peacetime standards of trim and finish by Duple. There were in fact 27 such new bodies, for the original ex-demonstrator TD1, No. 148, was also rebodied.

Two parallel series of Titans were built up in the early postwar years. Many more second-hand units came from an even wider variety of former users. In what might be called the recovery period, following the war, of shortages and general austerity, it was not easy to obtain new vehicles, and although some were acquired, the shortfall had to be made up with second-hand stock. Thus between 1946 and 1953 no fewer than 87 prewar double-deckers - 59 Leyland Titans and 28 AEC Regents - were purchased. They came from Leeds (three TD2s, fourteen TD5s and twenty AEC Regents), Leicester (three TD1s and five TD2s), Chesterfield (one TD2), Wigan (six TD1s and three TD4s), West Riding (two TD4s, nine TD5s and five TD7s), Barrow in Furness (two TD5c models), Todmorden (two TD5s), Hebble (one TD5), Plymouth (two TD4s), Burnley (one TD3), City of Oxford (seven AEC Regents) and London Transport (one AEC Regent). Whereas the 1940/1 second-hand vehicles had been bought under a deliberate Barton policy of having them rebodied before being used, the postwar influx were destined not to be rebodied.

Flanking all this second-hand activity was the intake of a large fleet of new Leyland Titan PD1s with Duple bodywork. Starting in 1947 and up to 1949 forty-two PD1s (some were the minor variant PD1A chassis - the difference related to types of suspension support) were put into service. From the mid 1950s Leyland PD2/12 and AEC Regent V chassis were bought new and there were second-hand vehicles gained as the result of buying other operators' vehicles, such as Allen, of Mountsorrel, in September 1955, which produced two Daimler CWA6 double-deckers as well as a PD1A and a PD2/1 Titan.

In 1957 a programme of rebuilding Leyland Tiger PS1 chassis from the late 1940s was undertaken. The refurbished chassis were rebodied by Willowbrook as 61-seat double-deckers with platform doors. There were nine of these and the exercise was repeated the following year when a further six Tigers were rebuilt and rebodied, this time by Northern Counties.

Direct second-hand purchases began again in 1958 with a postwar PD1 from Ribble and an ex-demonstrator AEC Bridgemaster. More refurbished

*Already by the mid-1930s (these pictures were taken in May 1935) Barton's headquarters boasted premises and maintenance facilities fully in keeping with the requirements of the then still very new 1930 Road Traffic Act, whose effects had not been felt until 1931. The first "modern" double-decker, No. **148 (TE 9520)**, the ex-demonstrator Leyland-bodied Titan TD1, is prominent, as are Leyland Lions No. **163 (VO 9463)** and **193 (AVO 193)**, respectively LT5 and LT5A models, the former with Leyland 35-seat and the latter with Willowbrook 39-seat coachwork. (Both: John Banks Collection)*

and rebodied single-deckers appeared in 1959, again bodied by Northern Counties and in that year second-hand TD4 and TD5 Titans came from Cumberland and PD1s from Preston and Wallasey (via an independent), Middlesbrough and Leicester.

Nineteen-sixty's AEC Regent Vs were fully fronted 70-seaters bodied by Northern Counties and there were more PD1s from Leicester, Western Welsh, Ribble and Birkenhead. In the following year perhaps the best known Barton double-decker appeared: the unusual lowbridge, low-height Dennis Loline, a Northern Counties 68-seater. The same coachbuilder also bodied six extended PD1 and PD2/1 chassis during 1961/2. In the early sixties, two former London Transport Craven-bodied RTs were among the 22-strong fleet acquired from Cream Bus Service, of Stamford, and Titans came from Yorkshire Woollen, St Helens, Chesterfield, Ribble, Todmorden, East Yorkshire and Crosville.

The last new double-deckers were six AEC Regent Vs in 1963 and then large numbers of ex-London Transport RTLs (and one RTW) made Barton look like an outpost of London Transport just as it had done of Leeds City Transport in the early postwar period. Barton thus ran examples of the Craven RT (ex-Cream Bus) and the RTL, an RTW, and even an STL, but

The family team that was making it all possible and, building on the foundations laid in the twenties and early thirties, taking the Company on to even greater things. From left to right, at Chilwell in May 1935, were Messrs Maurice, T H, Tom and Carl Barton: Maurice, Tom and Carl were respectively Works Manager, Chief Engineer and Traffic Manager. Thomas H's distinguished silver beard marked him out in any gathering; his other trade-mark - his peaked uniform cap - was for once being held in his hands. The Leyland was No. 2, a Bull chassis kitted out as a breakdown lorry. It had been new just over a year earlier. (John Banks Collection)

never a standard RT - strange when the huge numbers that flooded the second-hand market for PSVs is recalled.

The end of the Barton double-deck story came with five AECs: a lowbridge Regent III from Nottingham City Transport, two Renowns from Smith, of Barrhead (via Western SMT and a dealer), and two Regent Vs from City of Oxford in 1969.

There were to be no more: under the fleet replacement programme of the 1970s the finance was sought to sweep away the old régime and in its stead would appear a standardised fleet of Leyland Leopard and Bedford single-deckers. Thus the enthusiast was denied the sight of second-hand Routemasters or perhaps new Fleetlines and Atlanteans in Barton colours. And might there have been Bristol VRs once they became available on the open market? And Olympians? Pipe dreams...

This book has, as was Volume One, been made possible by the help over early vehicle details provided by Ron Maybray, who is once again thanked most warmly. The PSV Circle's publication PE8, dealing with the Barton fleet from 1960 to 1985, has also been helpful. Alan Oxley has again vetted the text and improved it considerably. David and Mary Shaw have read the proofs; the photographs were taken by Geoffrey Atkins unless stated otherwise in the captions. Finally, the usual disclaimer: this book offers neither a full history nor a fleet list of Barton's double-deckers. For that, and for the definitive and fascinating story of Barton, readers are urged to seek out copies of Alan Oxley's highly recommended three-volume history of the Company: Volume One published by the Transport Publishing Company and Volumes Two and Three by Robin Hood Publications.

John Banks
Romiley, Cheshire
February 2004

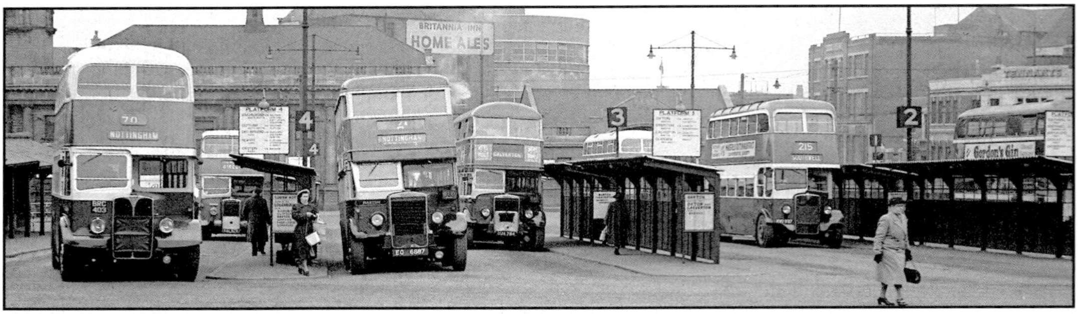

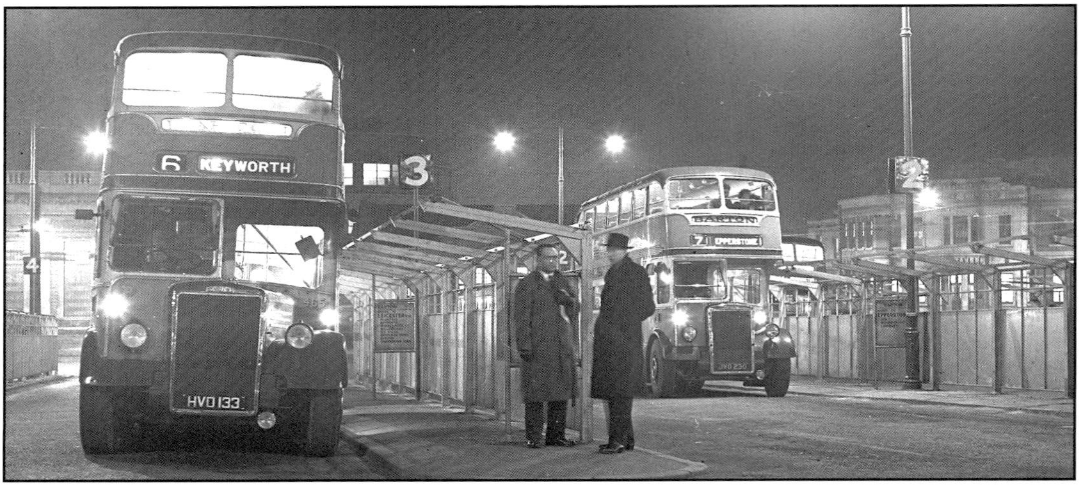

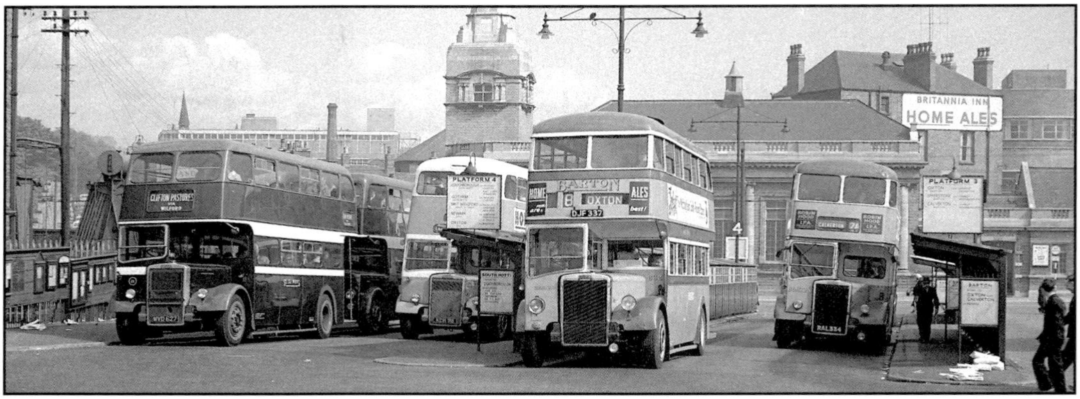

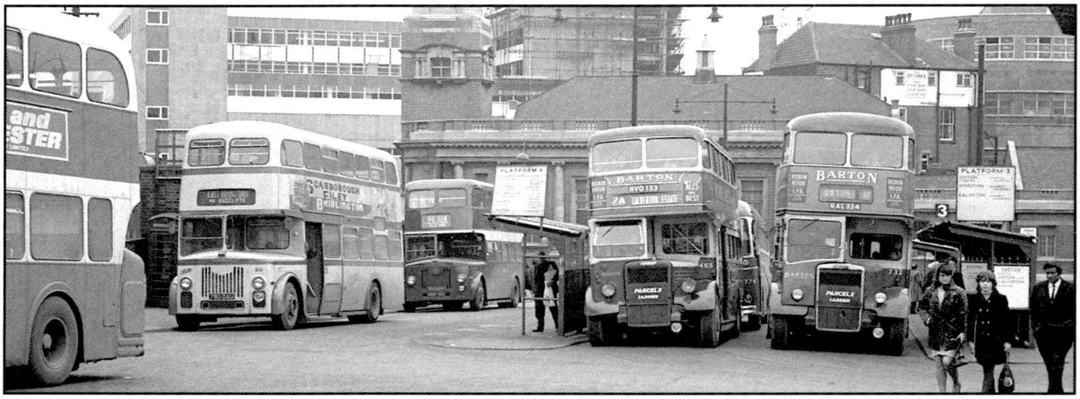

The Barton double-deck fleet 1932-69
A chronological survey

Above: But first ... here is an example of what answered the need for two decks before the era of the traditional typically British Barton double-decker began with No. 148, the Leyland Titan TD1 acquired in 1932. Gilford chassis were not common with double-deck bodies; they were light, fast machines more suited to express work, on which, indeed, perhaps the majority built were used. Barton, however, had five in 1929 that had double-deck bodies from earlier vehicles. Initially these were open-topped, later they had covered tops with open sides; this one - No. **33 (VO 1675)** - is seen in a further development where the upper-deck and its roof are more or less conventional. By 1931 it had become a normal, 32-seat, single-decker.

<< *Opposite page:* Before setting out on our 37-year odyssey among Barton's diverse and absorbing double-deck fleet, let us pause a moment to consider the Barton bus in its environment. Among Geoffrey Atkins's photographs are a few that are not specifically devoted to illustrating bodybuilder's products, but are expanded to make the bus take no more than its humble place in the streetscape. Those featuring Barton were usually taken at Huntingdon Street bus station, which was within easy distance of all of Geoffrey's homes in Nottingham over the years, and which he could pass if he chose as he walked into work in the morning or back home in the evening, or even pop out to at lunch time. They show buses and coaches in their topographical setting, usually with the vehicles of other local operators around. This quartet of such views is postwar and shows a selection of Barton Leyland Titans, some bought new, some second-hand ex-the Barrow, Leeds and Leicester municipalities, as well as Titans from the Trent, South Notts and Skills fleets, AEC Regents of Trent and Mansfield District and a Daimler in the fleet of Gash, of Newark. There is, too, a hint of the next generation in the shape of a rear-engined Trent Daimler Fleetline.

Upper: Number **148** (**TE 9520**), an ex-demonstrator TD1 with Leyland 48-seat lowbridge bodywork, was the first Barton Leyland Titan. *(John Banks Collection)*

Centre and lower: Although Barton took over many vehicles from acquired operators, double-deckers were in the minority, especially before the war. Notable in December 1935 were two AEC Regents from Campion, of Nottingham. Number **247** (**AAU 621**) was a 1934 Willowbrook-bodied lowbridge, forward-entrance 55-seater, seen in the centre view when brand new before delivery to Campion. The style of bodywork influenced Barton's later purchases of similar units. Number 247 was used in the Second World War to test the practicability of storing gas in a trailer as fuel for the bus during wartime petrol shortages, and the lower picture records that usage. *(John Banks Collection; Alan Oxley Collection)*

Upper: The other Campion AEC Regent had been new in 1930; **JF 223** was a highbridge 48-seater bodied by Ransomes and built to the design of the London General Omnibus Company's ST type. It is seen in Kent Street, Nottingham, before passing to Barton, with whom it took the fleet number 248.

Centre: Barton augmented their operation of double-deckers in 1939 with a batch of four new Leyland Titan TD5s with Duple lowbridge 53-seat bodywork. The forward-entrance arrangement as experienced on the ex-Campion AEC Regent AAU 621 was retained. The second of the four, No. **347** (**EVO 711**) was photographed at Ruddington in August 1940, complete with masked headlamps and white markings on the mudguards.

Lower: Nine more Leyland Titans, this time TD7s, came in 1940. Similar bodywork, seating 54, was ordered from Willowbrook and No. **374** (**FRR 148**) is shown.

Above: Number **371** (**FRR 145**), in later, rebuilt, condition, demonstrates the nearside aspect of the Willowbrook forward-entrance bodywork.

Below: A misty, murky May 1948 view at Huntingdon Street bus station, Nottingham, that neatly tells the story of Barton double-deckers of the early 1940s. Number **348** (**EVO 712**), another of the 1939 Duple-bodied TD5 Titans, stands alongside No. **421** (**FVO 322**), one of a pair of 1942 unfrozen AEC Regents with Northern Coach Builders lowbridge 55-seat bodywork. Behind are two 1943 Guy Arabs, with nearest the camera No. **430** (**GAL 389**). Nottingham's 1939 AEC Regent No. **31** (**FTO 614**) completes the group.

12

Above: Number **376** (**FRR 150**), the last of the 1940 Willowbrook TD7s, at Chilwell in August 1948 ahead of No. **393** (**VK 3841**), a 1930 Titan TD1 acquired from Tyneside Tramways in 1941. Barton had the vehicle rebodied by Duple as a lowbridge 55-seater before putting it into service.

Below: In a very fine image of wartime bus operation, Geoffrey Atkins caught No. **392** (**KR 6407**) in Bath Street, Nottingham, in June 1940. The headlamps are masked (with two different types of cover) and the sidelamp apertures are much reduced: both to lessen the chances of enemy bomber crews spotting the vehicle; and the front wings are partially painted white to help pedestrians to see the vehicle in the blackout. Note also the white markings on the kerb and the trolleybus traction pole in the background. A Leyland Titan TD1, the vehicle had come from Chatham and District Motor Services and was rebodied by Duple before entering Barton service.

Upper: Among the large number of second-hand Leyland TD1 Titans acquired in the early part of the war were four from London Transport. Number **413** (**GC 1212**) was one of three of them which came as chassis only, to be rebodied by Duple. It was at Mount Street, Nottingham, in June 1949.

Centre: The wartime utility Guy Arabs were no doubt welcome in those difficult times, but they were quite unlike anything previously operated by Barton. The first three came in 1942, followed by a batch of eight in 1943: all with Gardner 5LW engines. The lowbridge bodywork on those eleven came from four different coachbuilders: Brush, Northern Counties, Roe and Duple. Number **429** (**GAL 241**) was a 1943 Northern Counties example, seen here at Mount Street in September 1952.

Lower: The Roe utility bodywork is seen on No. **428** (**GAL 258**), also of 1943, photographed at Huntingdon Street in April 1956.

On this page are two views of 1943 Guy Arab No. **431** (**GAL 390**), a Duple-bodied example. The story of the wartime Guy Arabs is a complicated one that has by itself formed the subject of more than one full-length book. They came about as a result of the wartime Ministry of Supply drawing up a specification for both chassis and bodies that made maximum use of low-priority materials, i.e. those not needed for armaments production, and excluded curved profiles, thus avoiding skilled panel-beating work whose practitioners had gone to war in droves. Guy was the principle double-deck chassis builder, joined by Daimler and Bristol later in the war; bodywork was from a variety of coachbuilders, each of whom produced a design around the MoS specification that was nonetheless usually instantly recognisable. Operators had to apply to the Ministry of War Transport making out their case for new buses and that Ministry made the allocations. Barton received two more in 1944 and a further twelve in 1945. All Barton Guy Arabs had Gardner 5LW engines.

Above: The 1944 pair of utility Guy Arabs were bodied by Roe as lowbridge 55-seaters. Number **436** (**GNN 73**) was photographed in August 1947 at Huntingdon Street bus station.

Below: The twelve 1945 Guy Arabs were all bodied as lowbridge 55-seaters by Strachans. The angle chosen by the photographer for this view of No. **439** (**GNN 507**), at Broad Marsh bus station, Nottingham, in May 1953, emphasises the stark, upright, angular design of the body. The bonnet, designed to house either the five- or six-cylinder Gardner engine, protruded considerably, and this is also shown in this picture.

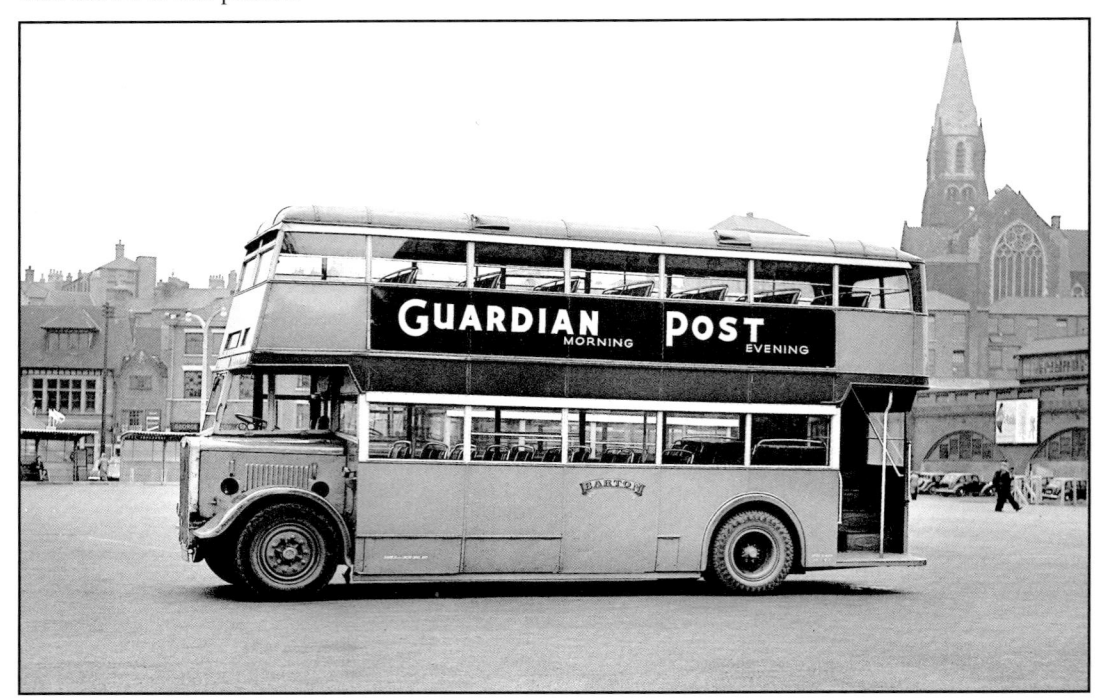

Above: Most users of utility Guys found that the bodies quickly deteriorated, mainly because of the use of unseasoned timber in their construction, but that the chassis remained sound. Many and varied were the ways of tackling that problem, from simply selling the vehicles (as did London Transport), through various degrees of rebuilding, to fitting them with completely new bodies. When Barton rebuilt the Duple body on No. **432** (**GAL 391**), the opportunity was taken to fit platform doors. The resulting vehicle was both attractive and workmanlike, as seen at Broad Marsh in April 1955.

Below: A similar rebuild, minus the platform doors, was applied to Strachans-bodied No. **440** (**GNN 544**), seen on the same day at Broad Marsh. Not all the Guys were rebuilt; unrebuilt examples were withdrawn from 1953 onwards, but the rebuilt vehicles lasted into the sixties, the last one going in 1966.

Above: Second-hand Leyland Titans from the earlier days of that model were to be a feature of Barton's purchasing policy for many years. In 1946 eight Brush-bodied 50-seaters came from Leicester Corporation: three 1931 TD1s and five 1932 TD2s. One of the TD1s, **JF 1532**, became Barton No. **476**, seen here alongside 1928 TD1 No. **399** (**AG 2529**), ex-Western SMT, and No. **478** (**RB 5507**), a Leyland-bodied 48-seat TD2 which came from Chesterfield Corporation in 1946. The ex-Western SMT vehicle had been rebodied by Duple upon acquisition by Barton in 1941.

Below: The first new postwar Leyland PD1 Titan chassis, delivered in 1947, was No. **455** (**HRR 942**), which was fitted with the 1942 Duple body formerly on withdrawn No. 411, one of the TD1s acquired from Tyneside in 1941. Number 455, photographed in June 1949, was withdrawn in 1952; its body was scrapped, and its chassis rebuilt as BTS1 single-decker No. 669.

Above: As the first half of a remarkable comparison of Leyland Titans that were entering the Barton fleet at around the same time in the late 1940s, Duple-bodied 55-seat lowbridge PD1 No. **464** (**JRR 932**) of 1948 is seen at Mount Street in May 1954. It was withdrawn in 1967.

Below: A few months earlier, in March 1947, six 1929/30 TD1s were purchased from Wigan Corporation. All were lowbridge 48-seaters, one bodied by Leyand, the others by Wigan's local coachbuilder, Massey Brothers, to Leyland design. One of the Massey vehicles, No. **503** (**EK 8110**), is seen at Mount Street in May 1949. It was withdrawn the following year.

Above: The Duple lowbridge Leyland Titan PD1s were part of the scene in Barton territory for two decades, their characteristic sliding doors, just forward of centre, and the aluminium body embellishments making them instantly recognisable. In a typical suburban scene, at Bramcote Avenue, Chilwell, No. **519** (**JVO 236**) was on the 18 Ilkeston - Beeston Rylands - Ilkeston circular service.

Below: Number **465** (**HVO 133**) features in one of Geoffrey Atkins's memorable night scenes at Huntingdon Street bus station. It was awaiting its departure time for Keyworth on service 6. In the backroud a 1938 Leyland Lion LT8 is on private hire duties.

Upper: The sliding doors more often than not tempted photographers to record the nearside of the Duple PD1s. Here is the equally attractive offside aspect, in a view of No. **580** (**KNN 254**) at the now vanished location of Granby Street, Nottingham, in 1956.

Centre: Rear views were even less often recorded, but on this occasion in 1969 at Chilwell No. **453** (**JNN 793**) tempted the photographer. The vehicle's condition and standard of presentation belied its 21 years. *(Ron Maybray)*

Lower: The last of the PD1s survived well into the 1970s. Number **512** (**JRR 261**) was a 1972 withdrawal; it is seen at Broad Marsh in October 1969. A number of detail changes affected the type over the years, including repositioning the registration number plate between the decks, the advertising on a panel at the foot of the radiator, and of course the Barton flag in place of the original winged cast motif. Numbers 453 and 512 are shown as rebuilt by Barton in 1959/60.

Above: One of the Duple-bodied PD1s, No. **510** (**JRR 752**), was in 1961 fitted with a second-hand Alexander 53-seat lowbridge body that had been carried by a Ribble Leyland Titan No. 2078 (RN 8643). This view of it dates from July 1964.

Below: The lure of second-hand Titans was still a strong one, even as the new Duple-bodied PD1s were coming on stream. As the years passed newer models became available and in 1949/50 Barton was able to buy a fleet of lowbridge TD4, TD5 and TD7 Titans dating from 1936-42 from the West Riding Automobile Company, all but two with Roe bodywork. Number **587** (**HL 7432**), a 1936 TD4, was the oldest. It was resplendent in its new Barton colours at Mount Street in August 1950.

Above: Typifying the ex-West Riding 1938 TD5s was No. **585** (**HL 8613**), again at Mount Street, in May of the same year. In the background were two more: Nos **584/3** (**HL 9057/9**).

Below: Barton No. **611** (**HL 9925**) was one of the TD7s, in this case one that had been new in December 1941. The vehicle ran for Barton until 1960. This picture of it was taken in August 1951 at Huntingdon Street.

In August 1950 a pair of 1937 Leyland TD5 Titans came from Barrow Corporation. Strictly, they were TD5c models (signifying torque-converter, an early form of clutchless automatic transmission), but they had been converted with conventional manual gearboxes before sale to Barton. The lowbridge bodies were 52-seaters constructed by English Electric. They survived only until 1954. In the picture above No. **609** (**EO 6886**) is illustrated at Mount Street, Nottingham, in October 1950. Some two years after its withdrawal it was converted into a transporter for the Barton Daimler replica, W 963. Number **610** (**EO 6887**) *(below)* was at the photographer's other favourite Barton location, Huntingdon Street bus station, in August 1952.

Another pair of 1938 Leyland-bodied lowbridge 53-seat TD5s were purchased later in 1950, in the November, from Todmorden Corporation. They entered Barton service, after overhaul and repaint, in January 1951. Geoffrey Atkins's offside/nearside pairing this time is of the same bus, No. **616** (**CWR 281**), which was photographed on different occasions (in the following March and June) at Mount Street working a service to Hillman Estate. The vehicle was 23 years old when withdrawn and scrapped in 1961. Its partner, No. 617 (CWR 289) went two years earlier.

The varied selection of second-hand prewar Leyland Titans continued in 1950 with the arrival of three 1936/7 TD4 models from Wigan Corporation. Lowbridge bodywork by Massey Brothers was fitted.

Upper: This view of No. **640** (**JP 1925**), a 48-seater that had been new in December 1936, was taken at Mount Street in September 1950.

Centre: The same vehicle in January 1951, alongside ex-West Riding Roe-bodied Leyland Tiger TS8 No. **601** (**HL 8213**).

Lower: Slightly newer, No. **642** (**JP 2028**) was a 55-seater dating from 1937, seen here in Barton livery in October 1950.

Above: Still in 1950, a solitary Roe-bodied lowbridge 53-seat Leyland Titan TD5 was acquired in October from Hebble Motor Services Ltd, of Halifax. The vehicle had been new to Hebble in November 1937 and was registered **JX 5729**. As Barton No. **628**, it was photographed in May 1951. It was withdrawn and scrapped in 1959.

Below: As a change from all the second-hand Leyland Titans, 20 AEC Regents were acquired from Leeds City Transport in 1950/1. All Roe-bodied highbridge 56-seaters, they had been new to Leeds in 1935-8. Number **661** (**CNW 910**) was a 1936 example, seen here in April 1956 after a repaint.

27

Above: New in November 1937, Barton No. **622** (**FNW 728**), had been No. 217 in the Leeds fleet. It came to Barton in November 1950 when exactly 13 years old and lasted a further seven years until withdrawal and scrapping in 1957. There is clear rear-end detail of ex-West Riding No. **611** (**HL 9925**), a 1941 Leyland Titan TD7. Both these vehicles had Roe bodies: 56-seat highbridge on the Leeds vehicle and 55-seat lowbridge on the West Riding. This is a June 1955 Mount Street view.

Below: The vehicle with the next fleet number, No. **623** (**FNW 736**) at the same place in the same month. Its Barton history was identical with that of No. 622.

Above: There were so many former Leeds vehicles in the Barton fleet that Nottingham became a place of pilgrimage for enthusiasts tracking them down. Two more of the AEC Regents appear in this November 1955 picture, led by No. **648** (**DUB 933**). A January 1937 delivery to Leeds, it was withdrawn and scrapped by Barton in 1960.

Below: Three AEC Regents came from City of Oxford Motor Services in June 1951. All had been new in August 1935 and were bodied as lowbridge 52-seaters by Weymann. Number **664** (**BFC 47**) was the first of them. It was photographed in February 1952 at Huntingdon Street.

Above: Just weeks into its new life with Barton, and freshly repainted, ex-City of Oxford **BFC 48** is seen running as Barton No. **665** at Huntingdon Street in September 1951. Although No. 664, seen in the previous picture, was withdrawn in 1954, No. 665 lasted into 1959 and the other one of the trio, No. 666, was converted in 1960 for operation as a tree-lopper and was scrapped in 1963.

Below: Four more former Oxford AEC Regents joined the Barton fleet in early 1953. Again lowbridge, this time they were East Lancashire-rebodied (in 1944) 51-seaters. Number **698** (**CFC 789**), which had been new in March 1936, was at Mount Street in October 1954.

Above: Closely following the former Leeds AEC Regents came a series of 1937/8 Leyland Titan TD5s from that municipality, some in late 1951 and the rest in early 1952. The earliest, according to the registration numbers, was **FNW 700**, new in October 1937, which became Barton No. **681**. It is seen at Broad Marsh in July 1956 and was withdrawn in 1961 and scrapped about two years later.

Below: **GUA 781**, an August 1938 vehicle, is seen as Barton No. **685** at Huntingdon Street in May 1952 not long after its repaint into Barton colours. The vehicle was withdrawn in 1959 and immediately scrapped.

Above: Four of the ex-Leeds Titans lasted into 1961 with Barton, and even they were outlived by two of the AEC Regents that survived into 1962, but most of them were withdrawn and scrapped in the late 1950s, including No. **682** (**FNW 702**), seen here in a quiet Huntingdon Street scene in May 1952.

Below: September 1953 found Geoffrey Atkins recording a similarly peaceful scene - perhaps these were Sunday photographs: although there are some pedestrians, again no other vehicles are visible. Former Leeds Titan No. **684** (**FNW 709**) is featured.

Above: To someone who, like the writer, was (and is) an especially keen follower of events in the London Transport fleet as well as that of Barton, the arrival in August 1953 of AEC Regent No. **699** (**DYL 838**) was of more than ordinary interest. A former member of the STL class, it had carried the bonnet number STL2186 in London. It had been new in September 1937 as a lowbridge 53-seater with body built by London Transport at Chiswick. Barton ran it until 1959 when it was scrapped. It had received its second Barton repaint a few days before this July 1956 picture was taken.

Below: A somewhat earlier - April 1954 - view of No. **699** illustrates well the Chiswick outline. Lowbridge STLs were very much in the minority and not many survived to run again in public service after London withdrew them.

Above: After the flood of second-hand double-deckers in the early 1950s, there were two new Leyland-bodied 58-seat lowbridge Titan PD2/12s, Nos 731/2 (RAL 333/4), which came in June 1954. As delivered, they had the traditional open-platform arrangement, as seen on the first of the pair, No. **731** (**RAL 333**), at Huntingdon Street in June 1955.

Below: In February 1959 the two PD2/12s were fitted with platform doors. In September 1967, a little farther back along platform 4 at Huntingdon Street, No. **731** again demonstrates. The bus had recently been repainted and had the "flag and Robin Hood" logo.

Above: The second of the pair was No. **732** (**RAL 334**), again seen in original condition, in an August 1955 photograph.

Below: A year earlier, in August 1954, this view of No. **732** emphasised the original layout of the open platform. Alongside was No. **723** (**RAL 38**), a 1954 Barton BTS1 that had been reconstructed from an earlier single-decker and rebodied as a 39-seater by Plaxton. The two Titan PD2/12s were withdrawn in April 1974 and both went on to find new owners, in 732's case albeit only as a play bus, but it did survive into preservation in 1984.

Above and below: Number **855** (**JDE 7**), a Leyland Titan PD1, which had been new in 1949 to Green's Motors, of Haverfordwest, passing to Western Welsh in 1956, came to Barton in March 1960. The upper picture was taken at Ilkeston Baths on Wharncliffe Road in April 1961 and the lower in December 1967 at Huntingdon Street. Number 855 was withdrawn in 1967.

Left: Among the vehicles acquired from Allen, of Mountsorrel, in 1955 was No. **755** (**CUT 857**), a 1945 Brush-bodied utility Daimler CWA6. It was withdrawn in 1957.

Upper: Here is **CUT 857** as Allen's No. **34** when brand new and on delivery from the coachbuilder Brush, of Loughborough, in April 1945. At that late stage of the war the bus was nonetheless equipped with masked headlamps, pinhole sidelamps and white wing tips. *(John Banks Collection)*

Centre: In addition to the Daimler CWA6 and another similar machine from Allen, there were two Leyland Titans (a PD1A and a PD2/1) and four single-deckers: again two Daimlers and two Leylands. The PD1A was **DUT 127**, which became Barton No. **753**. It had an Alexander 56-seat highbridge body built to Leyland's design and had been new in March 1947. It was photographed in Ilkeston Market Place in November 1955.

Lower: In a June 1959 view at Ilkeston Baths, the ex-Allen PD2/1 is illustrated. It had a Leyland 56-seat highbridge body. Number **754** (**GUT 455**) had been new in August 1951 and was withdrawn by Barton in July 1966. The PD1A outlasted it by six months, going in January 1967.

Above: In 1957 there appeared a further illustration of Barton's ability to produce new vehicles out of reconstructed earlier members of the fleet. Number **735** (**VVO 735**) was one of a batch of nine double-deckers thus created. Its chassis was that of Leyland Tiger PS1/1 No. 560 (KAL 380) of 1949, rebuilt and rebodied as a lowbridge 61-seater, with platform doors, by Willowbrook.

Below: Number **783** (**WAL 783**) was a similar rebuild. Its chassis had come from HPT 212, a Wilkinson, of Sedgefield, Leyland PS1. These pictures date from April 1958 and March 1957 at Mount Street and the buses were withdrawn in April 1974 and sold to dealers.

Above: Although new AECs had not been unknown in the Barton fleet, they played second fiddle to Leyland. The salesmen from Southall tried very hard, including offering the loan of Regent V demonstrator **88 CMV** in early 1955. It is seen in March of the year working on Barton's Calverton service.

Below: No doubt as a result of their experience with the demonstrator, Barton ordered two AEC Regent Vs for 1957 delivery. The first of them was No. **784** (**XAL 784**), seen here at Mount Street in October 1963. The 67-seat lowbridge body with platform doors was by Northern Counties.

Above: The second of the pair of 1957 Northern Counties-bodied lowbridge AEC Regent Vs was No. **785** (**XAL 785**). It was 15 years old when photographed at a modernised Mount Street bus station in November 1972, and would last another 2½ years before being withdrawn in May 1975.

Below: In 1958 there were further double-deckers utilising rebuilt single-deck chassis. The fifth of a batch of six was No. **790** (**XVO 790**), based on No. 552 (KAL 149), another 1949 Leyland Tiger PS1/1. The bodywork was again to lowbridge 61-seat specification, with platform doors, also by Northern Counties.

Above: The programme of double-deckers on reconstructed single-deck chassis continued into 1959 with a further ten examples, the first of which was No. **792** (**YRR 792**), a Northern Counties fully fronted forward-entrance 63-seater. The vehicle's origin was a Leyland Tiger PS1 chassis, JTB 459, from the Taylor, of Emneth, fleet. As a two-month-old double-decker it features in an August 1959 Mount Street scene and was withdrawn in September 1974.

Below: Number **795** (**795 BAL**) was a similar rebodied rebuild, yet another based on a Barton 1949 Leyland PS1/1, in this case No. 550 (KAL 147). This is a February 1967 picture.

Above: Another of the Northern Counties-rebodied single-deckers is seen in its first few weeks of service. Number **797** (**797 BAL**), new in August 1959, is seen at Mount Street in the September. This one was based on ex-Allen Leyland Tiger PS1 No. 759 (EJU 439).

Below: There was something different about No. **823** (**823 DNN**), the last of the ten 1959 rebuilt single-deckers, despite its resemblance to its contemporaries. It was described as a Barton BTD2, was a 70-seater and was based on a vehicle registered LAH 627 from Blue Coaches, of Shouldham. It was photographed at Derby bus station in April 1964 and withdrawn in March 1975.

Number **799** (**799 BAL**), another of those converted from a 1949 Barton PS1/1, in this case No. 561 (KAL 381), was in May 1963 fitted with a modified front panel arrangement featuring an AEC Regent grille. An ingenious touch, though Southall probably didn't think much to it, was the provision of an AEC-style triangular badge incorporating the word "LEYLAND". These are Mount Street pictures from August 1963.

Upper: Among the more interesting vehicles to be seen in the writer's home town of Kingston upon Hull in 1958 was an AEC Bridgemaster integral double-decker registered **76 MME**. In sharp contrast with Hull Corporation's bright blue and white colours, the livery of the Bridgemaster was the dignified combination of reds and cream used by Barton. It was thus no surprise when the vehicle joined the fleet in October 1958 as No. **805**. It remained in service until 1973. In this view it was at Regent Street, Nottingham, in June 1968.

Centre: The nearside aspect of No. **805**, at Mount Street in 1958.

Lower: The Bridgemaster at Derby on service to Nottingham. Air springs were nothing new in 1958, having been in use since before the war, but Barton thought it worth advertising that No. **805** was thus equipped. This was an early example of publicly extolling the features of a vehicle, a practice that proliferated on the back windows of coaches: videos, bars, kitchens, toilets, washrooms, and even happy drivers were thus proclaimed. In practice it simply meant that thieves watching coach parks were helpfully directed to the vehicles containing video players, and the gimmick died out.

Upper and centre: In mid 1959 a pair each of Leyland Titan TD4s and TD5s was acquired from Cumberland Motor Services. Dating from 1936 and 1938 respectively, all four had been rebodied with 1950 lowbridge 55-seat bodies by Eastern Coach Works. The first, according to the registration numbers, although with the highest Barton fleet number of the four, was TD4 No. **824** (**BRM 595**), seen *(upper)* at Broad Marsh in June 1960. Number **818** (**DAO 51**) *(centre)* was one of the TD5s. It was at Mount Street in August 1959. All four were withdrawn in 1964 (824) and 1965.

Lower: **HF 9598**, a 1946 Leyland Titan PD1, became Barton No. 819 on acquisition from Phillips Motor Services, of Holywell, in February 1959. Formerly with Wallasey Corporation, upon withdrawal in 1966 it was converted to tree-lopper No. **8**: as such it was at Chilwell in 1968 alongside No. **1038** (**CDJ 719**), an ex-St Helens Titan *(see pages 62/3)*, and No. **43** (**MVO 85**), a 1952 Barton BTS1 single-decker, seen as converted to a tanker in 1963. *(Ron Maybray)*

45

Above: Variety among the incoming second-hand Leylands was quite up to that of earlier years, and in October 1959 two former Middlesbrough Corporation PD1 Titans that had been new in June 1947 arrived. Number **828** (**XG 9304**) was withdrawn in 1971 and preserved by the writer's good friend Ron Maybray. At the time of writing it is at the Scottish Vintage Bus Museum, Lathalmond. This view of it dates from June 1961. The lowbridge 53-seat body was by Northern Counties.

Below: Another pair of mid-forties PD1 Titans, this time bodied by Leyland as 52-seaters, came from Preston Corporation in 1959. Number **807** (**BCK 938**), the newer of the two, was photographed in October 1962.

Above: In 1959/60 Leicester Corporation was withdrawing its 1946 Leyland-bodied Titan PD1 highbridge 56-seaters and no fewer than 16 passed into the Barton fleet. Number **831** (**DJF 336**) was a 1959 arrival and it was caught by the camera at Mount Street in March 1960.

Below: Among the 1960 intake was No. **848** (**DJF 351**), seen at Ilkeston in June 1960 two months after being licensed by Barton for further service. The ex-Leicester machines were withdrawn in the period 1965 to 1972. There cannot have been many other Leyland-bodied Titan PD1s still in service as the last of these Barton machines saw out their days in the early 1970s.

New chassis for double-deck bodywork in 1960 comprised a batch of five AEC Regent Vs, Nos 850-4 with matching reversed "FNN" registrations. The 70-seat bodywork was based on the familiar Northern Counties fully fronted forward-entrance design, although the frontal profile was curved and incorporated wrap-round windscreens and upper-deck front windows. Geoffrey Atkins chose No. **851 (851 FNN)** for his record of this batch. The photographs were taken at Mount Street in October *(above)* and June 1963. Number 851 was withdrawn from passenger-carrying service in 1973 and became the Barton driver-training vehicle. It is still owned by Barton. Three of the remaining four also went in 1973 and the last survived into 1974.

Among the considerable intake of early postwar Leyland Titans in 1960 was a solitary and rather unusual former Ribble example. **BRN 290** had entered service with Ribble in 1949, one of a batch of 30 on the Titan PD1/3 chassis fitted with Burlingham fully fronted 49-seat lowbridge bodies with platform doors. They were regarded as coaches and used on express services, especially to Blackpool. Known officially as "White Ladies" because of their livery, they were eventually reseated to 53 and repainted in Ribble's normal, dark-red livery: thereafter they were known to the enthusiast fraternity as "Red Ladies". This example was numbered **856** by Barton; it was withdrawn and scrapped in 1964. These photographs date from June 1960 and February 1961.

In a fleet as diverse and characterful as that of Barton, it might perhaps be difficult to single out any one vehicle - or batch of vehicles - as typical. There ought not to be much disagreement, however, as to which was the most unusual double-decker. Number **861** was a Leyland O.600-engined Dennis Loline. The Loline - an open market version of the Bristol Lodekka - was a low-height chassis that permitted standard seating on the upper deck within the overall height of a lowbridge bus. Barton ordered a 68-seat fully fronted forward-entrance body from Northern Counties that combined this facility with an actual lowbridge layout, thus achieving an exceptionally low overall height. Registered **861 HAL**, the vehicle was exhibited at the Commercial Motor Show in 1960 and was licensed for Barton service in April 1961. It was withdrawn in 1973, retained in preservation by Barton and still exists. In these July 1961 pictures, the still very new vehicle is seen in Huntingdon Street *(above)* and at Broad Marsh.

Above: Two Massey-bodied 56-seat highbridge PD1 Titans came from Birkenhead Corporation in April 1960. Number **858** (**BG 9222**) was the second of them and had been new in October 1946. It was at a wet and dreary Mount Street in October 1960.

Right and below: In September the following year seven similar vehicles were acquired from Birkenhead, in whose fleet they had been numbered 124/5/8-32 (BG 9678/7, ACM 303-7). Six, all shown here, were never used or given Barton fleet numbers and were dismantled for spares to keep the remaining early postwar Titans going. The seventh, ACM 303, was extended and rebodied by NCME as Barton No. 907.

Above: In February 1961 the business of Cream Bus Service, of Stamford, was acquired, bringing with it a mixed collection of AEC, Bedford, Commer and Ford chassis carrying a variety of coachwork. Of three AECs, two were ex-London Transport Craven-bodied RTs, KGK 731 and JXC 167, which Barton numbered 883/4. Number **884** (**JXC 167**) is seen in a September 1961 view at Ilkeston garage.

Below: Number **883** (**KGK 731**) was at Huntingdon Street in August 1961, alongside No. **906** (**HD 7838**), a 1948 Leyland PD2/1.

Above: The Titan PD2/1 No. **906** (**HD 7838**) had Brush highbridge 56-seat bodywork and had entered service in November 1948 with the Yorkshire Woollen District Transport Co. Ltd, of Dewsbury. It was initially sold to a dealer in January 1961 and passed to Barton the following April. It was run until only 1964 when it was scrapped by Barton at Chilwell.

Below: A remarkable purchase, as late as July 1961, was of an ex-Ribble 1939 Leyland Titan TD5, No. **918** (**RN 8608**). Admittedly this veteran had a postwar (1950) Alexander body, which may have helped it to outlive No. 906 by a year. It was sold for scrap in November 1965: a few years later it might well have been a candidate for preservation.

Above: The second-hand Leyland Titan contingent included three PD1s in July 1961. Lowbridge 53-seaters bodied by Weymann's Motor Bodies, of Addlestone, they had been new in November and December 1946 to the Chesterfield Corporation fleet. As Barton Nos 915-7, JRA 641/2/8 lasted in service until 1967. Number **917** (**JRA 648**) is seen at Mount Street in September 1961.

Below: In the same month No. **917** was photographed in the yard at Chilwell. Alongside was No. **66** (**593 FNN**), a 1960 Albion Claymore pantechnicon in Barton's lorry fleet.

Upper: Second-hand PD1 Titans from municipal fleets side by side in September 1961 at the bus station in Huntingdon Street, Nottingham: ex-Chesterfield No. **917** (**JRA 648**) and ex-Leicester **832** (**DJF 337**).

Centre: In December 1961 Eastern Coach Works bodies again reached the Barton fleet, this time with postwar chassis underneath them. Four 1947/8 Leyland PD1A Titan lowbridge 53-seaters, formerly in the Crosville fleet, were acquired through a dealer. The first, No. **919** (**GFM 912**), is seen in a view dating from May 1962.

Lower: Three Leyland-bodied lowbridge 53-seaters, acquired from Todmorden Corporation in early 1962, are represented by No. **943** (**FWT 184**) at Mount Street in June 1963.

The trio of ex-Todmorden PD2/1s were numbered **942**, **943** and **944** and registered **GWW 41**, **FWT 184** and **GWU 11**. All three are seen in pictures taken in Nottingham in May 1969 *(above)*, August 1962 *(left)* and April 1972 *(below)*, respectively at Broad Marsh, Mount Street and Regent Street. They were withdrawn in 1971 (944) and 1972.

Upper and centre: The former Todmorden PD2/1 Titans gave excellent value. A decade and a half old when bought by Barton, they gave good service for almost as long again (eleven years) before being withdrawn. In April 1968 at Huntingdon Street, No. **942** (**GWW 41**) was laying over between runs on service 7A and No. **943** (**FWT 184**) is seen at Broad Marsh.

Below: Given the number and variety of second-hand Leyland Titans in the Barton fleet, it was not difficult to find line-ups such as this one at Mount Street in May 1962. They were always worth recording on film and have, indeed, become symbols of the "old" British bus industry. This trio are Nos **830** (**DJF 335**), **918** (**RN 8608**) and **942** (**GWW 41**), respectively ex-Leicester, Ribble and Todmorden.

57

Perhaps ceding precedence only to the former Ribble "White Lady" for individuality in the ranks of Barton's second-hand Leyland Titans, No. **951** (**JAT 410**) was a 1947 PD1, formerly No. 442 in the fleet of East Yorkshire Motor Services Ltd, of Hull. Its obvious strangeness lay in the domed roof of its Roe 52-seat highbridge body, a feature for some decades provided on most of East Yorkshire's fleet in order that the vehicles might get into and out of the town of Beverley through the ancient stone arch at Beverley Bar. The arch is still, rightly, there, but development elsewhere in the town and consequent reroutings of the bus routes have done away with the need for special roofs, but for many years EYMS double-deckers were saddled with them, as was JAT 410 in further service with Barton. In these views it was at Mount Street in May 1963.

Above: One of Geoffrey Atkins's favourite spots for photography in Huntingdon Street bus station produced this picture of No. **954** (**CCK 362**), one of five ex-Ribble 1948 Leyland Titan PD2/3s acquired by Barton in the summer of 1962. Compared with the ex-Todmorden PD2/1s they were short-lived in Barton service, being withdrawn in 1966/7. In this May 1967 picture, therefore, No. 954 had not long to go before its last journey to the scrapyard.

Below: Another of the ex-Ribble quintet, No. **955** (**CCK 363**), was in Granby Street, Nottingham, in June 1963.

59

Above: Massive late-1960s redevelopment in the area of Mount Street bus station was making the place unrecognisable to those of us who had earlier made regular visits with the camera in search of Barton's latest acquisitions. In the frame on this occasion in June 1968 was a 1963 AEC Regent V, No. **961** (**961 PRR**), one of a batch of six 70-seaters with fully fronted forward-entrance bodywork of the by then familiar style from Northern Counties.

Below: The gradual shift towards ordering new AECs might have held out hopes of second-hand AECs in some numbers, but instead there was a large intake of Leyland RTLs from London Transport. One of the first, in December 1965, was No. **1034** (**OLD 648**), a 1948 Park Royal-bodied machine, seen at Ilkeston Market Place in February 1966.

Upper and centre: There were six RTLs in that first, December 1965, influx of former London Transport Leylands. A seventh vehicle, **KXW 441**, was an 8ft-wide RTW (the RTLs were 7ft 6ins wide). As Barton No. **1035**, it entered service without having been repainted, as seen in these views of it at Ilkeston garage in February 1966. Number 1034, illustrated on the previous page, was withdrawn in 1967 but the others, including the RTW, went in 1970-2.

Lower: Soon afterwards, sparkling in its new Barton colours, the RTW is seen at Ilkeston in 1969. *(John Banks)*

Upper and centre: Being a London Transport enthusiast, particularly if that involved following the fortunes of vehicles in further service after sale by LT, began in the 1960s to take on awesome proportions in regard to travelling around the country, as second-hand examples proliferated in further service with provicial operators. Those with Barton presented no problem, for the territory was already a regular location for visits. Number **1046** (**OLD 847**) *(upper)* was at Mount Street in January 1971 and in the following month No. **1108** (**LUC 25**) *(centre)* was tracked down in Ilkeston Market Place. Number 1046 was one of seven taken into stock in 1966; No. 1108 was one of eleven acquired in 1967. The ex-London Leylands were withdrawn in the period 1967 to 1972.

Lower: Alongside the ex-London RTLs in late 1965 were four Leyland PD2/9 Titans with highbridge 56-seat bodywork by D J Davies, of Merthyr Tydfil. They had been new to St Helens Corporation in 1954. Number **1039** (**CDJ 720**) was at Melton Mowbray in March 1968. All four were withdrawn later that year. *(John Banks)*

Upper: Here is the offside-rear aspect of the Davies bodywork, again as carried by No. **1039** (**CDJ 720**). This is another March 1968 photograph at Melton Mowbray. *(John Banks)*

Centre and lower: After all those ex-London and St Helens highbridge Leylands it seemed odd to find Barton buying a solitary lowbridge AEC Regent III in 1967. **SAU 199**, the former Nottingham City Transport No. 199, was a Park Royal-bodied 53-seater that had been new in April 1954. In the Barton fleet it took the fleet number **1087** and ran until withdrawal in 1972, when it went initially to a dealer and was then exported to the United States of America. In these photographs dating from May 1967 it was at East Circus Street, Nottingham. In the centre view can also be seen No. **969** (**969 RVO**), a 1963 Yeates-bodied Bedford VAL14, which - as a dual doorway, dual-purpose 56-seater - had three more seats than the double-decker.

Upper: In June 1968 two AEC Renowns dating from 1963, with Park Royal 74-seat front-entrance bodies, were acquired from a dealer. They had previously run for Smith, of Barrhead, and had passed to Western SMT in June 1968 but had not been used. The first of them, No. **1115** (**211 JUS**), is seen in Ilkeston in October 1969.

Centre: The last double-deckers to enter service with Barton were a pair of ex-City of Oxford 1958 Weymann-bodied highbridge rear-entrance 65-seat AEC Regent Vs acquired in December 1969. Number **1142** (**964 CWL**) was photographed in Ilkeston in July 1973 shortly before it and its partner No. 1143 (965 CWL) were withdrawn; No. 1142 became the Barton tree-lopper. When it was withdrawn from that duty, circa 1985, it was replaced by former Lincoln Corporation Leyland Titan PD2/31 tree-lopper KVL 684.

Lower: And here is the last of them all - the highest fleet number carried by a Barton double-decker was **1143**. The honour of bearing it fell to the other ex-City of Oxford AEC Regent V, **965 CWL**, seen at the modernised Mount Street in October 1970.